# ANIMALS ON THE BRINK

# Bottlenose Dolphins

Patricia Miller-Schroeder

www.av2books.com

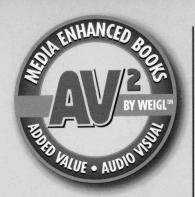

AV² provides enriched content that supplements and complements this book. Weigl's AV² books strive to create inspired learning and engage young minds in a total learning experience.

## Your AV² Media Enhanced books come alive with...

 **Audio**
Listen to sections of the book read aloud.

 **Key Words**
Study vocabulary, and complete a matching word activity.

 **Video**
Watch informative video clips.

 **Quizzes**
Test your knowledge.

Go to **www.av2books.com,** and enter this book's unique code.

 **Embedded Weblinks**
Gain additional information for research.

 **Slide Show**
View images and captions, and prepare a presentation.

### BOOK CODE

**S79005**

 **Try This!**
Complete activities and hands-on experiments.

**... and much, much more!**

**AV² by Weigl** brings you media enhanced books that support active learning.

Published by AV² by Weigl
350 5th Avenue, 59th Floor
New York, NY 10118
Websites: www.av2books.com    www.weigl.com

Library of Congress Control Number: 2013953035

ISBN 978-1-4896-0556-6 (hardcover)
ISBN 978-1-4896-0557-3 (softcover)
ISBN 978-1-4896-0558-0 (single-user eBook)
ISBN 978-1-4896-0559-7 (multi-user eBook)

Printed in the United States of America in North Mankato, Minnesota
1 2 3 4 5 6 7 8 9  17 16 15 14 13

122013
WEP301113

Project Coordinator Aaron Carr
Design Mandy Christiansen

Every reasonable effort has been made to trace ownership and to obtain permission to reprint copyright material. The publishers would be pleased to have any errors or omissions brought to their attention so that they may be corrected in subsequent printings.

Photo Credits
Weigl acknowledges Getty Images as its primary photo supplier for this title.

# Contents

## Take a Stand
### • Debate • Research •

# The Bottlenose Dolphin

For centuries, people who have lived near oceans have seen some very special animals. With their acrobatic leaps and curious faces, dolphins have always attracted human attention. Today, people who have never seen a dolphin in nature have probably seen one on television or at an aquarium or a zoo.

In this book, you will take an ocean journey to meet dolphins that race through water faster than an Olympic swimmer. Find out why some of these dolphins were once recorded traveling hundreds of miles (kilometers). Learn how they introduce themselves and how they play. Come see the wet world of the bottlenose dolphin and marvel at its acrobatic skills.

The bottlenose is the most familiar dolphin. Bottlenose dolphins are best known for their friendly look and playful nature.

A bottlenose dolphin seems to be always smiling because of the shape of its mouth. In fact, dolphins' faces are rigid and never change expression.

# How to Take a Stand on an Issue

Research is important to the study of any scientific field. When scientists choose a subject to study, they must conduct research to ensure they have a thorough understanding of the topic. They ask questions about the subject and then search for answers. Sometimes, however, there is no clear answer to a question. In these cases, scientists must use the information they have to form a hypothesis, or theory. They must take a stand on one side of an issue or the other. Follow the process below for each Take a Stand section in this book to determine where you stand on these issues.

1. **What is the Issue?**
   a. Determine a research subject, and form a general question about the subject.

2. **Form a Hypothesis**
   a. Search at the library and online for sources of information on the subject.
   b. Conduct basic research on the subject to narrow down the general question.
   c. Form a hypothesis on the subject based on research to this point.
   d. Make predictions based on the hypothesis. What are the expected results?

3. **Research the Issue**
   a. Conduct extensive research using a variety of sources, including books, scientific journals, and reliable websites.
   b. Collect data on the issue and take notes on all information gathered from research.
   c. Draw conclusions based on the information collected.

4. **Conclusion**
   a. Explain the research findings.
   b. Was the hypothesis proved or disproved?

# Dolphin
# Details

The biggest bottlenose dolphins are about as long as two full-grown people and weigh about as much as seven large humans.

The largest bottlenose dolphins live in Moray Firth, Scotland. They need more layers of fat than other dolphins to survive the cold temperatures of the North Sea.

# Features

There are about 40 **species** of dolphins living in the world's oceans. Dolphins are actually small toothed whales. Bottlenose dolphins are fairly large compared to other dolphins.

Dolphins may look like fish in many ways, but they are **mammals**. They share many features with land mammals such as cows, dogs, humans, and hippopotamuses. Dolphins breathe air and are warm-blooded. They give birth to live babies that drink milk from their mothers' bodies. Dolphins have special adaptations to help them live in their watery world.

Bottlenose dolphins vary a great deal in size. How big they grow seems to depend on where they live. Large dolphins are better at staying warm than small dolphins are. They are also better at diving deep to catch food. Some large-bodied dolphins are able to store more oxygen in their blood. Because of these adaptations, large bottlenose dolphins live in the colder, deeper regions of the oceans. Smaller bottlenose dolphins live in warm oceans or close to shore in shallow water. These different-sized bottlenose dolphins belong to the common bottlenose dolphin species. They are called **ecotypes** because the way they look depends on where they live.

The largest recorded bottlenose dolphins live in the cold, deep waters around the British Isles. There, males grow to almost 13 feet (4 meters) and females to more than 10 feet (3 m). The big males can weigh more than 1,400 pounds (635 kilograms). In the warm waters off Florida's coast, both males and females are between 8 and 8.5 feet (2.4 and 2.6 m) long and weigh between 420 and 570 pounds (190 and 260 kg). In the warm, shallow water of Shark Bay off northern Australia, bottlenose dolphins reach only 6.5 feet (2 m) in length.

On average, female bottlenose dolphins live longer than males do. Researchers working with dolphins in nature estimate females often live more than 40 years and males about 25 to 30 years. The oldest female bottlenose dolphins are more than 50 years old. Researchers think males face more danger and stress during the mating season, when fights and chases can occur.

# Classification

Dolphins belong to a large group of animals called the Cetacea. *Cetacea* comes from a Latin word that means "large sea animal." There are about 85 species of dolphins, whales, and porpoises that belong to this group. They swim in oceans around the world.

There are two basic types of Cetaceans. They are **baleen** whales and toothed whales. Baleen whales have enormous mouths that are filled with long strips of baleen. These strips work like a huge sieve to strain small creatures from the water. Some of the largest ocean creatures, such as the blue whale, use baleen to filter and eat the smallest ocean creatures. The baleen whales make up only 14 Cetacean species. Many of them are **endangered** or **threatened**.

Most Cetaceans are toothed whales. These whales include mighty sperm whales, which can dive more than 2,100 feet (640 m), and river dolphins, which are almost blind and live in the murky waters of the Amazon, Ganges, and Yangtze Rivers. River dolphins are among the most endangered of the Cetaceans. Other toothed whales include porpoises, killer whales, and bottlenose dolphins.

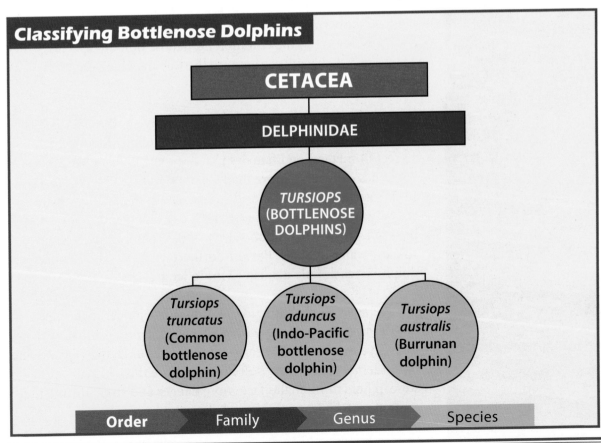

The best-known dolphin species is the common bottlenose dolphin. It is sometimes called the Atlantic bottlenose dolphin.

The Indo-Pacific bottlenose dolphin is usually longer and more slender than the common bottlenose dolphin.

The largest member of the Delphinidae family is the killer whale. It can weigh more than 10,000 pounds (4,500 kg).

# Special Adaptations

Most mammals live on land, where the air they need is easily available. Bottlenose dolphins are mammals with many adaptations that help them live in the world's oceans.

## Blowhole

A bottlenose dolphin has a large nostril called a blowhole on top of its head. The animal breathes out stale air from its lungs through the blowhole. Then, fresh air full of oxygen is brought in through two valves underneath the blowhole. The blowhole is often closed. The dolphin must open it when at the water's surface in order to breathe out and in.

## Snout

The bottlenose dolphin gets its name from the shape of its head and snout, which some people think resembles a bottle. Bottlenose dolphins have a rounded forehead that is separated from their snout by a crease. This unusual forehead contains fat and is called the melon because of its shape. The melon helps the dolphin push through the water when swimming.

## Streamlined Body

Its **streamlined**, torpedo shape lets the dolphin glide easily through water at speeds of more than 27 miles (43 km) per hour. Its skeleton is long, narrow, and flexible. Even its head, with a smooth, pointed snout and gently rounded forehead, pushes easily through the water.

## Fins and Flippers

Like fish, dolphins have a **dorsal fin** on their backs. This fin is made of sturdy tissue. The dorsal fin helps the dolphin swim in a straight line through the water. Dolphins have flippers, which are smooth, slim fins that help them steer underwater.

## Blubber

Dolphins have a smooth layer of fat, called blubber, under their skin. A thick layer of blubber helps the bottlenose dolphin remain comfortable swimming and living in cold oceans. Blubber is also an effective way to store food energy.

## Flukes

Bottlenose dolphins' tails are both rigid and flexible. The tail lies horizontally and is made up of two halves, called flukes. Flukes move up and down instead of side to side like a fish tail. The up-and-down movement gives a powerful push through the water.

# Senses

Just like humans, dolphins have senses of sight, touch, smell, taste, and hearing. They have an additional special sense that helps them "see" using sound. This sense is called **echolocation**.

Bottlenose dolphins must adjust the pupils in their eyes quickly from bright light at the water's surface to dim light below. Strong muscles around their eyes let them change the shape of their lenses to focus. Bottlenose dolphins focus on an object with two eyes as humans do. Still, they often turn on their side and look with only one eye. Dolphins can move each eye independently, giving a wide range of vision.

Dolphin skin is very sensitive to touch. Bottlenose dolphins swim close together, using their skin to communicate. Water pressure on their skin helps dolphins adjust to swimming at different depths. The skin around the blowhole, especially sensitive to pressure, lets dolphins know when they can breathe at the surface without taking in water. Sensitive skin on dolphins' lower jaws helps them feel objects they want to investigate.

Bottlenose dolphins do not have a good sense of smell. The blowhole often has to remain closed because the dolphin is underwater. When the blowhole is open, it is busy exchanging stale air for fresh. The time the dolphin has available to test for smells is very limited.

Dolphins use their sense of taste. They appear to have taste buds on their tongues. These taste buds let the dolphin taste many substances that have dissolved in the water. The tastes can help the dolphin find food or mates.

Bottlenose dolphins have excellent hearing. The streamlined dolphin has no external ears, just tiny ear holes behind the eyes. In bottlenose dolphins, the ear holes are only 0.1 inch (2.5 millimeters) wide. Their lower jaws contain oily fat that stretches toward their middle ears. Sound waves hit the lower jaw and collect in the fat. The fat channels the sound waves to the middle ears inside a dolphin's head.

Dolphins echolocate by making a series of rapid clicking sounds. As many as 1,200 clicks per second are turned into a beam of sound waves. When the beam hits an object, an echo bounces back. The fat in the dolphin's lower jaw picks up the echo, which contains information about the object's size, shape, speed, and even texture.

# Dolphin
## Details

When a bottlenose dolphin breathes deeply, it takes in more oxygen than a human does. This means dolphins do not have to breathe as often.

Dolphins and other toothed whales are the only marine mammals that have developed echolocation. Bats use a form of echolocation on land.

# Dolphin
# **Details**

Bottlenose dolphins often mimic, or copy, the sounds or actions of dolphins and other creatures they meet.

Indo-Pacific bottlenose dolphin groups are found in coastal waters around South Africa, throughout the Indian Ocean, and near Southeast Asia and Australia.

# Groups

**B**ottlenose dolphins are social animals. More is known about the social activities of these dolphins than many other Cetaceans. Bottlenose dolphins were among the first dolphins to be kept in aquariums. They are still the ones visitors are most likely to see in a zoo or an aquarium. This accessibility has allowed researchers to study their social interactions up close. However, captivity can sometimes change how animals behave. Social groups in an aquarium may not be what a dolphin would choose in nature.

To find out more about bottlenose dolphins, researchers have studied the social behavior of dolphins living in nature. Some studies have gone on for many years. One thing these studies show is how adaptable bottlenose dolphins are. Their social groups are affected by many things in the environment, including the depth of the water, the type of food available, and the number of **predators**.

Bottlenose dolphin groups have been known to vary in size from 2 to more than 1,000 members. The larger groups are usually a loose-knit community containing many smaller social groups. These small groups are usually called pods or schools. Certain dolphins seem to stick together, but others leave and rejoin pods at will.

Mothers and their young, which are called calves, are often found in groups with other mothers whose calves are close to the same age. Adult females seem to have close ties with other female relatives. This means that pods of adult females often contain mothers, daughters, sisters, grandmothers, and aunts. This type of social group is called a **matriline**.

Adult males seldom join female groups except for short periods to breed. When male calves become **juveniles**, they start to form groups away from their mothers. As the males mature, they often form close friendships or alliances with one or two other males. These allied males can be close companions for many years. Juvenile females often join groups of other young dolphins, although some stay with their mothers. Most females return to their mother's group as they get older.

In bottlenose social groups, some dolphins are dominant. These animals have a higher position in the group. Large, adult males are usually the most dominant. They sometimes chase, bite, slap, or ram other dolphins. By making sure everyone knows their high position, these dolphins can get the most or best food or a better chance to mate.

# Communication

Dolphins share certain signals and behaviors that are important for communicating. Young dolphins learn these behaviors by watching their mothers. The young dolphins also watch other adults in the group.

Bottlenose dolphins use many different sounds when vocalizing. Researchers who have placed microphones underwater have heard clucks, squawks, croaks, barks, wails, whistles, clicks, and creaks. Dolphins make these sounds through their blowholes.

Bottlenose dolphins have a unique way of introducing themselves. Each dolphin has its own signature whistle, which seems to be like a name. When a dolphin gives its signature whistle, another dolphin will often repeat it. Perhaps this is a way of showing that the second dolphin recognizes the whistler. It could also be a welcome. Having a signature whistle seems important to being part of a dolphin social group.

Touching and rubbing are important parts of bottlenose dolphin communication. Touching flippers seems to be a friendly greeting when two dolphins meet. A dolphin that uses its flipper to touch another's side between the dorsal fin and fluke seems to be asking for something, such as food, a toy, or a massage. Rubbing bodies together, or with a flipper, may show affection.

Play seems to be an important part of dolphin social behavior. Bottlenose dolphins of all ages play both together and alone. Groups or pairs of dolphins practice acrobatics such as leaping, spinning, and tail stands. They spit water and splash with flippers and flukes. They ride the surf or other waves together.

Play behavior can sometimes be hard to tell from fighting. Both activities include chasing, slapping, biting, and ramming. Researchers think that dolphins approach each other from behind or slightly from one side when playing. They also roll over and rub each other when play-fighting. In real fights, there is no rolling or rubbing, and opponents usually approach head to head or at right angles. Playing dolphins make loud whistles and whines. They may expel, or send out, small streams of bubbles from their blowholes. Fighting dolphins give loud squawks and expel large clouds of bubbles.

# Dolphin
# **Details**

The bottlenose dolphin has up to 108 small cone-shaped teeth.

Dolphins do not have vocal cords like humans. They make noises by adjusting air sacs under their blowholes.

# Body Language

Animals often use body language to communicate with other members of their species. Flippering is one example. Sometimes, a dolphin lies on its side, raises a flipper above the water's surface, and slaps the water several times. Scientists believe the animal is signaling danger, aggression, or play to other dolphins. A bottlenose dolphin uses its head, tail, and flippers to communicate in many different ways.

## Spyhopping

Dolphins often stick their heads above the surface of the water. This is called spyhopping and lets the dolphins have a look above the water's surface. They may be checking to see where other dolphins are and what they are doing, or they may be curious about a boat or some other object.

## Breaching

When a dolphin leaps out of the water and lands with a splash, it is breaching. This is often done when other dolphins are nearby, so breaching may be a signal or another form of communication. Many young dolphins start breaching when they are only a few weeks old.

## Lobtailing

Lobtailing is when a dolphin raises its tail flukes out of the water and splashes them down on the surface. This may have more than one purpose. Dolphins may use lobtailing to signal others or to show aggression.

## Synchronized Displays

Sometimes, two bottlenose dolphins swim so close together that their bodies almost touch. They move together like synchronized swimmers. The pair may breach, move their flippers, spit water, or lobtail exactly together. It is usually two male bottlenose dolphins doing these displays. Perhaps they are letting other males know that they are a team. The display may also be a way to attract females.

### Take a Stand
·Debate·
·Research·

### Should aquariums continue to keep dolphins in captivity?

Many aquariums feature bottlenose dolphins. Some of these dolphins have been born in captivity, but many have been captured in nature. Aquarium dolphins educate visitors and often thrill them by performing in shows. However, there is concern that keeping the animals in captivity harms them.

#### FOR

1. Keeping dolphins in aquariums allows people to observe them up close. Seeing ocean mammals in this way encourages people to care about the marine environment.
2. A great deal of research in aquariums is difficult to do in natural **habitats**. Aquarium animals help scientists learn more about their behavior and needs.

#### AGAINST

1. Most dolphin pools in aquariums are too small for a fast-swimming animal that uses echolocation and travels freely in nature.
2. Captive dolphins generally have shorter life spans than those recorded for dolphins in nature. Dolphin calves born in aquariums have less chance of surviving infancy.

# Dolphin
# Details

During pregnancy, a bottlenose female will often rest her large belly on soft underwater sand.

Bottlenose dolphin calves are usually born tail first so they do not drown.

# Mating and Birth

Bottlenose dolphins usually breed and give birth from late spring to late summer. Timing varies depending on where they live. During this time, single males or male pairs visit female groups looking for mates. Sometimes, the males will separate a female from her pod and stay with her for a few hours or even a few weeks. While with her, they will chase away any other males who come too close. Often, both males in a pair will breed with the female. Either one could be the father of her calf. After mating, the males leave the female in search of other mates. Pregnant females return to their pods.

**Gestation** in bottlenose dolphins takes 12 months. Females gain about 100 pounds (45 kg) during pregnancy. The birth season is usually at a time when calves have the best chance to survive. This is often when there is the most food or when there are fewer predators. Females may move into safer nursery areas before giving birth. Nursery areas are often shallow and close to shore, where there are fewer sharks.

Bottlenose dolphins almost always give birth to a single calf. In captivity, births are usually at night and last anywhere from 45 minutes to several hours. Once it is born, the calf quickly swims to the surface for its first breath. The mother, or another female called an aunt, pushes the newborn bottlenose dolphin to the surface if it needs help.

## From an Expert

*"I study individual dolphins for months or even years. After watching the dolphins for so much time, I get to know each one very well. Every dolphin has a distinct personality, just like people do—some are relaxed, some are careful, and some are bossy."* Amy Samuels

Amy Samuels (1951–2008) worked as a biologist with the Chicago Zoological Society and the Woods Hole Oceanographic Institution in Massachusetts. She studied the behavior of bottlenose dolphins at the Brookfield Zoo in Illinois. She also studied bottlenose dolphins in nature at Shark Bay off the northwest coast of Australia.

# Calves

Many mammals are helpless when they are born. On land, the mothers of helpless infants can keep them hidden in dens or carry them to safety. Dolphin calves must be alert and able to swim from birth, however. They have to swim to the surface to breathe and follow their mothers through the ocean. Calves need to learn many skills to survive and to be part of a dolphin pod.

Bottlenose dolphin calves are **precocious**. This means their eyes are open and they can swim and follow their mothers from birth. However, a calf still depends on its mother and swims close by her side. Predators, such as sharks, look for young dolphins away from their mothers. These calves are easy prey.

Mothers produce a rich high-fat milk. Newborns nurse for a few seconds at a time, several times an hour both day and night. Calves grow quickly on this high-fat diet. Even so, the calf needs its mother to feed and protect it for at least two years.

Bottlenose calves often touch their mothers with their flippers to keep contact when swimming. Sometimes, calves ride on their mother's bow wave and coast along beside her. A bow wave forms on both sides of a dolphin as it moves forward in the water.

During their early years, young dolphins have much to learn from their mothers. Mothers teach their calves about finding food, avoiding predators, and communicating with other dolphins. Teaching communication skills begins with the signature whistle. A mother repeats her signature whistle over and over to her newborn. This helps the young dolphin find its own mother if the two become separated. Even in a large group, the calf will recognize its mother's signature.

A young dolphin also has to learn its own signature whistle. Mother bottlenose dolphins choose a whistle for their calves and then coach them in practicing it over and over. This is similar to a human parent naming a child. The parent then helps the child learn to use its name to identify itself.

A newborn dolphin has a few hairs on its snout that soon disappear. All mammals have hair at some point in their development.

# Dolphin
# **Details**

Female bottlenose dolphins have given birth to calves when they were 40 years old.

Mothers and their calves have a strong bond. The calves stay close to their mothers and depend on them for food and protection.

# Dolphin
# Details

Bottlenose dolphins shed and replace their outer layer of skin every two hours. That is nine times more often than human skin is replaced.

A popular activity for juvenile bottlenose dolphins is riding the waves created by boats and large whales. This is called bowriding.

# Development

At birth, a bottlenose dolphin is about 45 inches (115 centimeters) long. This is about half as long as its mother. For such a big calf to fit inside its mother before birth, it must be crumpled up. This leaves several lines on its sides called fetal folds. The folds disappear as the calf grows. Dorsal fins and flippers are bent at birth but straighten out after a few days. An average calf weighs about 40 pounds (18 kg) at birth. This is about 10 percent of its mother's weight.

The calf grows rapidly and is smooth, sleek, and playful. By 4 months of age, most calves are playing with and eating small fish. Calves know their signature whistles by 1 year of age. By 2 years, most calves are no longer drinking mother's milk. They are able to feed themselves. Still, some calves nurse for up to four more years. Play is very important. It allows calves to practice their hunting, predator-defense, and social skills. As they get older, they spend more time away from their mothers, but a calf still comes to its mother for protection and comfort.

Dolphins who are between 3 and 8 years old are juveniles, a stage similar to a human teenager. Many leave their mothers to spend time with groups of other juveniles. Juvenile females may stay with their mothers longer than males. At some point, most juveniles join a group that contains youngsters from 3 to 13 years old. These groups can be quite rowdy, with plenty of social and physical activity.

Many females have their first calf when they are between 8 and 12 years old. Very young mothers have a more difficult time raising a calf. Most young mothers return to their mother's pod or may join a pod of other mothers with calves. Other females this age stay in the juvenile group but may visit their mother's pod.

Males between the ages of 8 and 13 years are busy forming bonds with one or two other males in the juvenile group. They will be friends and allies for many years, perhaps their whole lives. Eventually these young males leave the juvenile group. Male pairs travel around visiting other pods. Most will not breed successfully until they are 20 years old.

# Habitat

**B**ottlenose dolphins are very adaptable. They are able to live in a wide variety of marine habitats. Coastal-living dolphins can be found in harbors, bays, lagoons, and river mouths that open into the oceans. Offshore-living bottlenose dolphins do equally well in the deep oceans far from shore.

Bottlenose dolphins are one of the most widespread of all groups of dolphins. They live in all of the world's warm and **temperate** oceans and coastal areas. They are found as far north as Norway, Nova Scotia in Canada, northern California, and northern Japan. They can also be found as far south as Chile and the southern tips of New Zealand, Argentina, and South Africa. Bottlenose dolphins are found in many inland seas such as the Black, Red, and Mediterranean.

## Organizing the Ocean

Earth is home to millions of different **organisms**, all of which have specific survival needs. These organisms rely on their environment, or the place where they live, for their survival. All plants and animals have relationships with their environment. They interact with the environment itself, as well as the other plants and animals within the environment. These interactions create **ecosystems**.

Ecosystems can be broken down into levels of organization. These levels range from a single plant or animal to many species of plants and animals living together in an area.

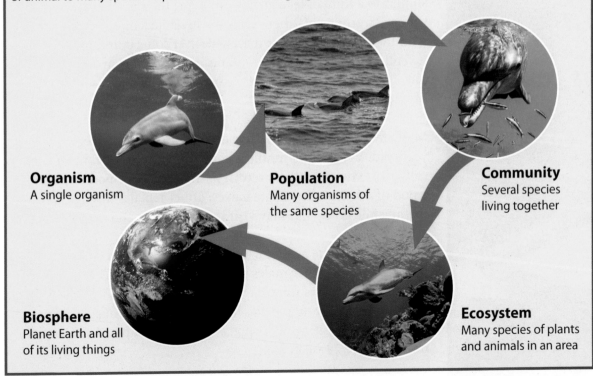

**Organism**
A single organism

**Population**
Many organisms of
the same species

**Community**
Several species
living together

**Biosphere**
Planet Earth and all
of its living things

**Ecosystem**
Many species of plants
and animals in an area

The only places bottlenose dolphins cannot be seen doing their acrobatic leaps are the frigid polar seas.

Dolphins have to think about breathing, so they cannot sleep as humans do. They rest with one eye open and half of their brain active at all times. If they forget to take a breath at the surface, they can suffocate or drown.

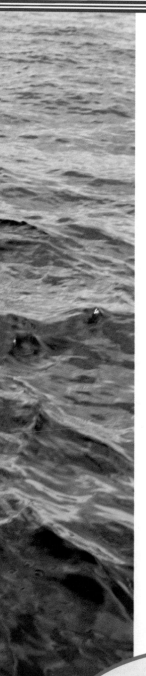

# Migration

**M**any groups of bottlenose dolphins spend their lives within a local community. Several **generations** of one social group may be found close together. These groups of dolphins seldom **migrate** very far.

Some dolphin groups migrate long distances. They may migrate to follow food sources or to search for mates. Even local groups may move if their food is affected by the tides or seasons. Males may travel farther during the breeding season, when they are looking for mates. Scientists believe offshore-living dolphins may migrate farther than those that stay in communities close to shore. Offshore groups are not as easy to follow and study.

A big change in the environment can make a long migration necessary. In 1983, the weather and currents in the Pacific Ocean near South America changed. Colder water moved north, causing food shortages for marine mammals as far north as California. A group of bottlenose dolphins that lived near San Diego moved north. The dolphins followed the fish they usually ate. In two to three months, the dolphins swam more than 400 miles (645 km) to Monterey Bay in northern California. It was the longest recorded migration for bottlenose dolphins. When the weather returned to normal, some dolphins traveled south. Others chose to stay in their new home.

## From an Expert

Kathleen Dudzinski has studied the social behavior and communication of bottlenose dolphins in Japan. Her research was featured in the IMAX film *Dolphins*. She is the director of the Dolphin Communication Project.

*"Once we learn to recognize what is acceptable to dolphins—what they consider 'good manners'—then we can better manage how we observe and interact with dolphins, whales, and other marine life. We must learn to respect them as the wild animals they are."*
Kathleen Dudzinski

# Diet

Bottlenose dolphins are carnivores. That means they hunt and eat other animals. The type of animals they eat depends on what species are found in the habitats they call home. In general, bottlenose dolphins are fond of eels and other fish, squid, octopuses, and crustaceans, such as crabs and lobsters.

Bottlenose dolphins eat a variety of animals. Scientists studied the stomachs of bottlenose dolphins that had been stranded on shore and died. They contained the remains of 72 different prey species. An active adult bottlenose dolphin needs to eat 15 to 30 pounds (7 to 14 kg) of food each day.

Bottlenose dolphins have many ways to catch a meal. Sometimes, a dolphin hunts alone, using its snout like a shovel to dig in the sandy bottom of shallow warm waters. This activity, sometimes called bottom grubbing, helps a dolphin find small fish hiding in the sand. Another hunting method is fish whacking. In this technique, a powerful whack from a dolphin's tail fluke sends fish flying up to 30 feet (9 m). The dolphin then feeds on the stunned fish at the water's surface. Snacking is another method used by dolphins hunting alone. A dolphin swims upside down near the surface, chasing a small fish. When close to the fish, the dolphin opens its mouth, twists around, and catches its prey.

Groups of bottlenose dolphins do some of the most spectacular hunting. Several dolphins cooperate in chasing or herding fish. Fins or flukes slapped on the surface help them herd. They sometimes form a circle around the fish, driving them to the surface where they become trapped. Some researchers think dolphins may use echolocation to stun fish with sound waves.

In narrow tidal creeks, bottlenose dolphins sometimes drive fish out of the water onto muddy banks. The dolphins beach themselves on the mud, grabbing fish before wiggling back into the water.

The age of a bottlenose dolphin shows in its teeth. The teeth have a layer of enamel for each year of growth, similar to growth rings in trees.

Salmon, mullet, and catfish are favorite foods for many bottlenose dolphins.

# The Food Cycle

**A** food cycle shows how energy in the form of food is passed from one living thing to another. Bottlenose dolphins are higher up the food cycle than plants or animals that eat plants. However, bottlenose dolphins are not at the very top of the food cycle because there are other carnivores that eat them. In the diagram below, the arrows show the flow of energy from one living thing to the next through a **food web**.

**Producers**
Tiny plants called **plankton** live in the ocean and use sunlight to produce food energy.

**Tertiary Consumers**
Bottlenose dolphins feed on fish, squid, and other creatures such as octopuses and crustaceans.

**Primary Consumers**
Small, shrimplike krill eat plankton in the water.

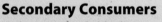

**Secondary Consumers**
Fish, squid, and baleen whales feed on krill.

### Apex Predators
Bottlenose dolphins are hunted and eaten by sharks.

### Decomposers
When a bottlenose dolphin dies, decomposers break down its body materials. This adds nutrients to the ocean that help plankton to thrive.

### Parasites
Bottlenose dolphins provide a home for parasites such as tapeworms, roundworms, and flatworms.

## Take a Stand
· Debate ·
· Research ·

### Should bottlenose dolphins receive more protection?

The International Union for Conservation of Nature (IUCN) lists the common bottlenose dolphin as a species of least concern. That means the species has a fairly low risk of becoming **extinct** compared to threatened or near threatened species. The status of the Indo-Pacific bottlenose and the Burrunan dolphin species is not determined, however.

#### FOR

1. The Marine Mammal Protection Act of 1972 protects bottlenose dolphins in U.S. waters. It is illegal to hunt, harass, capture, or kill marine mammals there. The bottlenose dolphins that live outside the United States need protection as well.
2. Bottlenose dolphins may be plentiful in some areas today, but long-term conservation of all their environments around the world is required in order for them to survive.

#### AGAINST

1. Governments and conservation groups have time and money to protect only the species most at risk. They cannot treat every species as endangered.
2. Additional protection for bottlenose dolphins might have a financial cost to the world's commercial fishers and tourist industry.

Some studies show that older dolphins may make calming sounds to resolve conflict in a pod.

# Competition

Earth's oceans are the bottlenose dolphin's home. This may seem like a vast place full of room to move and food to eat, but like all animals, bottlenose dolphins sometimes compete with each other for food or mates. Dolphins also compete with other animals, including humans.

Bottlenose dolphins often cooperate when hunting, but sometimes they fight over the same food. When groups of dolphins feed around fishing ships, the dominant males get their pick of the fish thrown overboard. Younger males, females, and calves get what is left. Adult male bottlenose dolphins often compete for females. Males who are friends cooperate with each other to get females but compete with other single or paired males. Fights can occur during competition.

Bottlenose dolphins are frequently found in areas where other dolphin species live. Sometimes, the different species avoid competing by using different habitats or eating different foods. Sometimes, they use the same habitat and food but eat at different times. If a food source is large, such as the fish thrown from a commercial boat, several species can eat together with few problems. Bottlenose dolphins that live in shallow waters usually do not compete with those that live in deep, offshore areas.

Groups of bottlenose dolphins have been seen chasing and attacking harbor porpoises. They do not eat the porpoises. The reason the dolphins attack them is not clear.

Bottlenose dolphins, especially young males, use their teeth to make marks on the backs of other dolphins when fighting or playing. The marks are temporary.

# Dolphin
## Details

Echolocation is a very useful tool for finding the way in a dark ocean. It is also a good way to find food, predators, and other dolphins that are at a distance.

Australian pelicans and bottlenose dolphins in Western Australia cooperate while fishing. They herd the fish into a tight ball close to the shore, where it is easier to capture them.

# Bottlenose Dolphins with Other Animals

Bottlenose dolphins share the oceans with many different kinds of creatures. Some of these animals provide food for dolphins. Dolphins also sometimes provide food for other larger creatures, such as killer whales.

Bottlenose dolphin skin is usually dark gray on the back, fading to pale cream or pinkish gray on the belly. Dark backs help camouflage dolphins, making it harder for predators to see them. The dolphins' pale bellies blend in with the lighter surface water to help them hide from predators swimming below.

Some creatures feed on bottlenose dolphins without killing them. A species of small sharks called cookie cutters takes small but deep bites out of living dolphins. These bites leave deep, round scars. Many bottlenose dolphins have scars from encounters with larger sharks, as well. Dolphins do not always lose in a shark encounter. Groups of bottlenose dolphins can ram and kill sharks to protect calves or other companions.

Bottlenose dolphins have fairly peaceful relations with other large dolphin species. They are sometimes found in mixed groups with spinner or spotted dolphins far out in the ocean. Bottlenose dolphins have peaceful relations with large baleen whales as well.

In some places in the world, bottlenose dolphins cooperate with humans to catch fish. Off the coasts of Australia, Mauritania, Brazil, and Spain, certain groups of dolphins seem to have special relationships with human fishers. These relationships may be centuries old. On cue from humans, the bottlenose dolphins herd fish toward shore. The humans catch fish in their nets, and the dolphins are able to catch fish that escape the nets.

# Folklore

Since ancient times, dolphins have captured people's imaginations. As they leaped from the waves, dolphins seemed to represent the power of the mysterious ocean. In ancient times, taking the life of a dolphin was as serious a crime as taking the life of a person.

Images of dolphins appeared in the artwork of ancient Greece, Rome, and Crete, beginning more than 3,000 years ago. In Greek legends, dolphins were related to the gods. Dolphins guided Poseidon, the god of the sea. His son, Triton, was half-man and half-dolphin.

Dolphins have been part of the legends and stories of many ancient people who lived near the oceans. The Chumash people, who live in what is now California, have a legend explaining how dolphins and people are related. Dolphins were formed when some of the earliest people fell into the ocean and were drowning. The Earth goddess turned them into dolphins to save their lives. The Chumash see dolphins as brothers and sisters of their people.

The ancient peoples of New Zealand and Australia also had legends about dolphins. They believed dolphins were messengers from the gods. In their stories, their ancestors took the form of dolphins to guide boats and rescue others. In New Zealand, from 1888 to 1912, a dolphin regularly escorted ships through a narrow and dangerous channel called Pelorus Sound. Pelorus Jack is credited with saving many sailors from ending up on the dangerous rocks. After thousands of tourists came to see Pelorus Jack, the New Zealand government passed a law to protect him.

A sculpture of dolphins stands along the sidewalk around the harbor of Muscat in Oman.

| Myth | **VS** | Fact |
|------|--------|------|
|  Bottlenose dolphins always live in harmony with other members of their species. | | Dolphins often help or defend a pod member, but they can also be aggressive and fight, bite, or chase each other. |
|  Dolphins are always friendly to people. | | There are true stories of dolphins helping people who are drowning or threatened by sharks. Dolphins in nature are untamed animals, however, and should not be approached closely or touched by those who do not understand their behavior. Some dolphins may be aggressive when feeding or mating and may see humans as threats. |
|  Dolphins, which eat huge numbers of fish, are causing the disappearance of fish that humans catch for food. | | Bottlenose and other dolphins have almost been wiped out in some areas because of this myth. Human fishers are more likely to take too many fish than dolphins are. Pollution also kills fish needed by both dolphins and humans. |

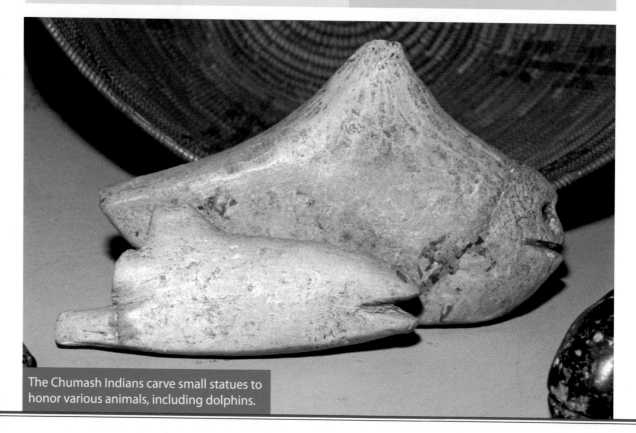

The Chumash Indians carve small statues to honor various animals, including dolphins.

# Status

**B**ottlenose dolphins are found in oceans and along coastlines throughout the world. Although they are not considered endangered, they live in a vulnerable environment that is rapidly becoming polluted. Toxic substances that are in the water as a result of human activity are harming many types of fish that dolphins eat. Bottlenose dolphins are adaptable, but they cannot leave the ocean. Their future is linked to the future of the oceans.

Dolphins and whales are slow breeders. They do not have large litters of young like many land animals or fish. They give birth to one calf and spend several years feeding and protecting it. If many bottlenose dolphins start to die, their populations will have a hard time recovering.

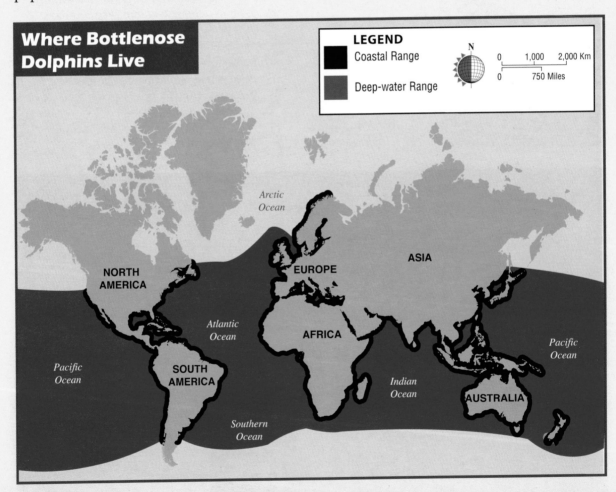

**Where Bottlenose Dolphins Live**

**LEGEND**
Coastal Range
Deep-water Range

N

| 0 | 1,000 | 2,000 Km |
| 0 | 750 Miles | |

Human activity causes several problems for bottlenose dolphins. Dolphins are exposed to many harmful chemicals from industry that seep into the oceans. Some of these chemicals dissolve in fat. They become concentrated in the blubber of dolphins and other marine mammals. This can make the animals very sick. The poisons can even be passed on to dolphin calves through their mother's milk.

Drift nets are another human-caused problem for bottlenose dolphins. Drift nets are sheets of thin netting that drift with the ocean current or tide to catch huge numbers of fish. Some of these nets are 30 miles (48 km) long. Air-breathing marine mammals, such as bottlenose dolphins, that get caught in them risk suffocating. The large number of fish caught can also reduce the dolphins' food supply.

Commercial and recreational boats can threaten the safety of dolphins. Many bottlenose dolphins carry scars or have mangled dorsal fins or flukes from boat propellers. These injuries can affect the ability of dolphin groups to survive. Noise pollution from motorboats and jet skis can interfere with dolphin echolocation and socializing.

Some children and adults on tour boats or from shore enjoy feeding dolphins in nature. This pleasurable activity is illegal in U.S. waters, however. It is a threat to the safety of humans and dolphins alike.

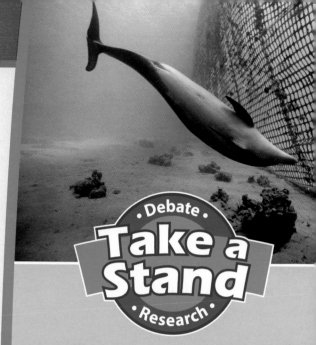

## Take a Stand

·Debate· ·Research·

### Should nets that accidentally catch bottlenose dolphins be outlawed?

Many nets used for legal fishing can accidentally kill or injure dolphins. A range of fishing gear, including drift nets and shrimp **trawls**, catch other types of marine life besides the fish being hunted.

#### FOR

1. In areas such as the Black Sea, local populations of bottlenose dolphins are declining because fishers see them as competition. In the past, fishers have also killed dolphins for their meat.
2. Until there is a penalty for accidentally catching bottlenose dolphins, the practice will continue.

#### AGAINST

1. Commercial and local fishing industries in the world's oceans would experience financial hardship if they were not able to fish in the easiest, most inexpensive ways possible.
2. Bottlenose dolphins are not an endangered or threatened species. Laws regulating industry and possibly reducing food supplies for people should be reserved for protecting the animal species most at risk.

# Dolphin
# **Details**

Some people think dolphins and porpoises are the same animal, but they are in different families. A dolphin has a longer snout, a bigger mouth, more curved fins, and a longer body.

Staff members at the Sarasota Dolphin Research Program released a bottlenose dolphin in Tampa Bay, Florida, in 1990, after two years of studying the animal in California. Researchers there studied the dolphin's echolocation abilities and behavior patterns.

# Saving the Bottlenose Dolphin

The Sarasota Dolphin Research Program (SDRP), which was founded in 1970, is the longest-running study of bottlenose dolphins in nature. The SDRP, which operates in Sarasota Bay, Florida, was supported originally by Mote Marine Laboratory and now by the Chicago Zoological Society. The organization's cofounder and director, Randall Wells, began studying this population of dolphins as a high school student.

Since the organization's founding, SDRP scientists, interested students, and Earthwatch volunteers have worked together to identify more than 4,800 different dolphins over five generations. The program has tracked and studied dolphins in the Sarasota Bay area using the markings on their dorsal fins. This work has led to a greater understanding of the biology and behavior of coastal bottlenose dolphins. The results of the various studies will help lead to the development of sound resource management policies. The program's overall missions are dolphin research and conservation, as well as educating people about dolphins.

## From an Expert

Randall Wells is a conservation biologist with the Chicago Zoological Society and cofounder and director of the Sarasota Dolphin Research Program in Florida. He has published many articles on his work with bottlenose dolphins.

*"We are trying to learn about the natural lives of wild dolphins, so questions arise about whether to interfere when a dolphin is stranded or injured. I'm not completely resolved about this but humans do harm the dolphin community, so it seems right to compensate, to give some injured or sick dolphins a second chance."*
Randall Wells

# Back from the Brink

Dolphins and whales are fascinating animals that are affected by human activity in many ways. In 2013, for example, hundreds of bottlenose dolphins along the mid-Atlantic coast of the United States washed up on shore, dead or dying from a measles-related virus. The virus does not infect humans. A dolphin's only protection against the virus is its natural ability to build **antibodies**.

The National Oceanic and Atmospheric Administration (NOAA) responded to the alarming outbreak by providing funds to investigate possible causes. Researchers suspect a lung infection possibly made worse by a polluted coastal ecosystem. Bottlenose dolphin populations are able to withstand the outbreaks, which appear to occur in cycles. About 800 of the species died from a similar virus in the late 1980s.

There are ways to protect the world's bottlenose dolphins. You can learn more about these animals by contacting many conservation organizations, including the American Cetacean Society. You can get informed about the latest news, support research about bottlenose dolphins, or help pay for the care of a single dolphin. A school class or individual may "adopt" an animal, receiving a color photo, details about the animal's life, and other conservation information from zoos, aquariums, or research organizations. For more information about the American Cetacean Society or supporting a dolphin through the Sarasota Dolphin Research Program, contact:

**American Cetacean Society**
P.O. Box 1391
San Pedro, CA 90733

**Sarasota Dolphin Research Program**
c/o Chicago Zoological Society
3300 Golf Road
Brookfield, IL 60513

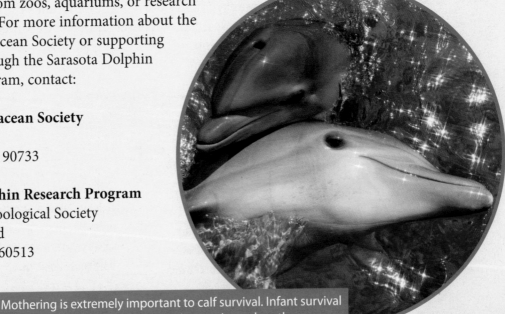

Mothering is extremely important to calf survival. Infant survival is much lower with very young or inexperienced mothers.

# Activity

**D**ebating helps people think about ideas thoughtfully and carefully. When people debate, two sides take a different viewpoint on a subject. Each side takes turns presenting arguments to support its view.

Use the Take a Stand sections found throughout this book as a starting point for debate topics. Organize your friends or classmates into two teams. One team will argue in favor of the topic, and the other will argue against. Each team should research the issue thoroughly using reliable sources of information, including books, scientific journals, and trustworthy websites. Take notes of important facts that support your side of the debate. Prepare your argument using these facts to support your opinion.

During the debate, the members of each team are given a set amount of time to make their arguments. The team arguing the For side goes first. They have five minutes to present their case. All members of the team should participate equally. Then, the team arguing the Against side presents its arguments. Each team should take notes of the main points the other team argues.

After both teams have made their arguments, they get three minutes to prepare their rebuttals. Teams review their notes from the previous round. The teams focus on trying to disprove each of the main points made by the other team using solid facts. Each team gets three minutes to make its rebuttal. The team arguing the Against side goes first. Students and teachers watching the debate serve as judges. They should try to judge the debate fairly using a standard score sheet, such as the example below.

| Criteria | Rate: 1-10 | Sample Comments |
|---|---|---|
| 1. Were the arguments well organized? | 8 | logical arguments, easy to follow |
| 2. Did team members participate equally? | 9 | divided time evenly between members |
| 3. Did team members speak loudly and clearly? | 3 | some members were difficult to hear |
| 4. Were rebuttals specific to the other team's arguments? | 6 | rebuttals were specific, more facts needed |
| 5. Was respect shown for the other team? | 10 | all members showed respect to the other team |

# Quiz

**2.** Do male or female bottlenose dolphins tend to live longer?

**3.** What is echolocation?

**1.** How many species of oceanic dolphins are there?

**5.** What is it called when a dolphin raises its tail flukes out of the water and splashes them down on the surface?

**6.** How long does gestation take for bottlenose dolphins?

**4.** How many members are in a bottlenose dolphin pod or school?

**9.** Why are dolphins called carnivores?

**8.** Where is the only place bottlenose dolphins cannot be seen?

**7.** How much does the average dolphin calf weigh?

**10.** How does noise pollution affect bottlenose dolphins?

**Answers:**
1. about 40 2. Female bottlenose dolphins live longer than males. 3. the ability to focus and bounce sound waves off objects 4. 2 to more than 1,000 members 5. lobtailing 6. 12 months 7. about 40 pounds (18 kg) 8. in the frigid polar seas 9. because they hunt and eat animals 10. It interferes with echolocation and socializing.

# Key Words

**antibodies:** substances made in the body and found in the blood that can act against a virus

**baleen:** long strips that are found on the upper jaw made up of tough, flexible material similar to horns

**dorsal fin:** a raised ridge on the back of a dolphin or whale

**echolocation:** the ability to focus and bounce sound waves off objects

**ecosystems:** communities of living things and resources

**ecotypes:** animals from one species with different sizes and appearances, depending on their environment

**endangered:** a type of plant or animal that exists in such small numbers that it is in danger of no longer surviving in the world or in a certain area

**extinct:** no longer surviving in the world or in a certain area

**food web:** connecting food chains that show how energy flows from one organism to another through diet

**generations:** typical lengths of time between birth of parents and birth of their children

**gestation:** the carrying of the young inside its mother's womb

**habitats:** places where animals live, grow, and raise their young

**juveniles:** not fully grown or developed animals

**mammals:** warm-blooded animals that have hair or fur and nurse

**matriline:** a group made up mainly of related females, such as mothers, daughters, and aunts

**migrate:** to make a regular, seasonal movement to a different region

**organisms:** forms of life

**plankton:** floating and drifting tiny organisms in the sea

**precocious:** unusually advanced or mature in development

**predators:** animals that live by hunting other animals for food

**species:** groups of individuals with common characteristics

**streamlined:** having a smooth, torpedo shape that allows animals to glide easily through water or air

**temperate:** having moderate temperatures

**threatened:** at risk of becoming endangered

**trawls:** large cone-shaped nets that drag along the sea bottom to catch marine life

# Index

# Log on to www.av2books.com

AV² by Weigl brings you media enhanced books that support active learning. Go to www.av2books.com, and enter the special code found on page 2 of this book. You will gain access to enriched and enhanced content that supplements and complements this book. Content includes video, audio, weblinks, quizzes, a slide show, and activities.

## AV² Online Navigation

**Audio**
Listen to sections of the book read aloud

**Book Pages**
AV² pages directly correspond to pages in the book.

**Video**
Watch informative video clips.

**Key Words**
Study vocabulary, and complete a matching word activity.

**Embedded Weblinks**
Gain additional information for research.

**Quizzes**
Test your knowledge.

**Slide Show**
View images and captions, and prepare a presentation.

**Try This!**
Complete activities and hands-on experiments.

---

**AV² was built to bridge the gap between print and digital. We encourage you to tell us what you like and what you want to see in the future.**

## Sign up to be an AV² Ambassador at www.av2books.com/ambassador.

Due to the dynamic nature of the Internet, some of the URLs and activities provided as part of AV² by Weigl may have changed or ceased to exist. AV² by Weigl accepts no responsibility for any such changes. All media enhanced books are regularly monitored to update addresses and sites in a timely manner. Contact AV² by Weigl at 1-866-649-3445 or av2books@weigl.com with any questions, comments, or feedback.